AF506133

THE MYSTERY SCHOOLS

Grand Relief of Eleusis:
Demeter, Triptolemos, and Persephone
5th century BC

The Mystery Schools

Grace F. Knoche

A Sunrise Library Book

THEOSOPHICAL UNIVERSITY PRESS
PASADENA, CALIFORNIA

A Sunrise Library Book

Theosophical University Press
Post Office Box C
Pasadena, California 91109-7107
www.theosociety.org/pasadena
1999

Originally published in 1940 by Theosophical University Press

Second & Revised Edition

This book is printed on acid-free paper

Library of Congress Cataloging-in-Publication Data

Knoche, Grace F.
    The mystery schools / Grace F. Knoche. — 2nd & rev. ed.
        p.   cm.
    Includes bibliographical references and index.
    ISBN 1-55700-066-2 (pbk. : alk. paper)
        1. Mysteries, Religious.   2. Theosophy.   I. Title.

BL610 .K6 1999
299'.934—dc21   99–045623

Printed at Theosophical University Press
Pasadena, California

Contents

Foreword

A Mystery school is a university of the soul, a school for the study of the mysteries of the inner nature of man and of surrounding nature. By understanding these mysteries, the student perceives his intimate relationship with divinity, and strives through self-discipline and devotion to become at one with his inner god.

This book attempts to present certain fundamental lines of teaching which it is hoped will give a more or less clear picture of what a Mystery school really is. Full and specific knowledge of the Mystery schools — where they have been, where now they function, what are their chief characteristics — has not been given out. Modern historians of the Greek mystery centers, for example, marvel at how well the rule of secrecy imposed upon the candidates was kept. This does not pertain to the public aspect, such as the fourteen-mile procession along the Sacred Way from Athens to Eleusis in which men, women, and children participated. But "the rites of the Greater Mysteries . . . the true secrets of the *teletai* [initiation proper] and the *epopteia* [the culminating vision] have never been divulged."*

The student can find, however, a generous amount of information scattered here and there in the literatures of the past and can build up for himself a coherent picture of the pageantry of the Mystery schools, a picture which will turn into the reality of experience only as he becomes inwardly prepared through lifetimes of dedication and the study and practice of the ancient wisdom.

That which can be discovered by the sincere student may be likened to our knowledge of the atom. Who, for example, has ever seen the *real* atom? What microscope has penetrated the secret of its existence? Yet today we know more about the atom with its electrons than has been revealed for centuries. Although invisible to both eye and lens, scientists have detected the *flash of its track*, its "way of light"; through diligent and painstaking labor they have studied this way of light until, through inference and evidence, the structure of the atom and its components, its almost spiritual origin, has been revealed.

Thus with the Mysteries: as we look at the pages of history, and further into the mist of unrecorded time,

---

*Mircea Eliade, *A History of Religious Ideas* 1:294.

we do not see the schools themselves, but through study and devotion we may glimpse the flash of their track, their way of light. From inference and spiritual testimony we can trace the pageantry of the light-bearers as they have passed from age to age, inaugurating the grand religions and philosophies of the human race. Some of these lights shine with immense glory, others with less strength, while still others are but fitful gleams of half-understood truth.

The physicist cannot point to the physical atom, yet he knows it exists as the basis, the foundation, of all matter; the student of theosophy cannot show you a Mystery school, yet he knows it exists as the heart or atomic center of the spiritual and intellectual life of the planet. Who then would dare assert the non-existence of the Mysteries, of this potent atom of esotericism, when luminous traces of spiritual power are seen scattered all over the world? If our physical bodies are rooted in invisible fiery lives, why should not our human spiritual, intellectual, and moral bodies likewise have their origin in the spiritual and intellectual fire-mist of the planet?

An uninterrupted history of the occult network of the human race is not available to us today, for such records are the guerdon of the pledged disciple, but with the powerful lens of the ancient wisdom we can study the way of light flashed forth by each lightbearer over the centuries; can recapture the atmosphere of the ancient temples; can discern the purpose of the schools, their methods of teaching; and, last but not least, can learn of the strong discipline imposed upon the candidates seeking initiation into the knowledge of their secret origin and their still more secret destiny.

The author's debt to theosophy as presented by H. P. Blavatsky cannot be measured. One can only hope that the present study will encourage those new to her writings to drink deep of the springs at their source.   — G. F. K.

Pasadena, California
October 2, 1999

THE MYSTERY SCHOOLS

Seek this wisdom by doing service, by strong
search, by questions, and by humility; the wise who see
the truth will communicate it unto thee, and knowing
which thou shalt never again fall into error. . . . There
is no purifier in this world to be compared to spiritual
knowledge; and he who is perfected in devotion find-
eth spiritual knowledge springing up spontaneously in
himself in the progress of time.

— *Bhagavad-Gītā* 4:34–5, 38
(Judge Recension)

Chapter 1

Founding of the Brotherhood

M ILLIONS UPON MILLIONS of years ago in the darkness of prehistory, humanity was an infant, a child of Mother Nature, unawakened, dreamlike, wrapped in the cloak of mental somnolence. Recognition of egoity slept; instinctual consciousness alone was active. Like a stream of brilliance across the horizon of time, divine beings, mānasaputras, sons of mind, descended among the sleeping humans, and with the flame of intellectual solar fire lighted the wick of latent mind, and lo! the thinker stirred. Self-consciousness wakened, and man became a dynamo of intellectual and emotional power: capable of love, of hate, of glory, of defeat. Having knowledge, he acquired power; acquiring power, he chose; choosing, he fashioned the fabric of his future; and the perception of this ran like wine through his veins.

Knowledge, more knowledge, and still greater knowledge was required by the maturing humans who looked with gratitude to the godlike beings who had

come to awaken them. For many millennia they followed their guidance, as children lovingly follow the
footsteps of their mother.

As the ages rolled by, a circulation of divine instructors succeeded these primeval mānasaputras and
personally supervised the progress of child-humanity:
they initiated them in the arts and sciences, taught
them to sow their fields with corn and wheat, instructed them in the ways of clean and moral
living — in short, established primeval schools of
training and instruction open and free to all to learn
of things material, intellectual, and spiritual. At this
early period there were no Mystery colleges: the
ancient wisdom was the common heirloom of all
mankind, for as yet there had been no abuse of knowledge, and hence no need for schools kept hid and
sacred from the world. Truth was freely given and as
freely accepted in that golden age. (Cf. H. P. Blavatsky
Collected Writings 14:248–9.)

The race was young; not all were adept in learning. Some through past experience in former world
periods learned quickly and with ease, choosing intuitively the path of spiritual intellection; others, less
awake, were good though wayward in progress; while
a third class of humans, drugged with inertia, found
learning and aspiring a burden and became laggards in

the evolutionary procession. To them, spiritual apathy was preferable to spiritual exertion.

Mankind as a whole progressed rapidly in the acquisition of knowledge and its subsequent use. Some obviously wrought evil — others good. What had been latent spirituality now became active good and active evil. Suffering and pain became nature's most merciful method of restoring the heart to its primeval instinct, that of spiritual choice. As mind developed keener potentialities and the struggle for mental supremacy overcame the spiritual, the gift of intellect became a double-edged weapon: on the one hand, the bringer of spiritual awareness and undreamed of intellectual ecstasy; and on the other, the wielder of a weapon of destruction, of horror and, in the worst cases, of deliberate spiritual wickedness — diabolism. As H. P. Blavatsky wrote:

> The mysteries of Heaven and Earth, revealed to the Third Race by their celestial teachers in the days of their purity, became a great focus of light, the rays from which became necessarily weakened as they were diffused and shed upon an uncongenial, because too material soil. With the masses they degenerated into Sorcery, taking later on the shape of exoteric religions, of idolatry full of superstitions, . . .
>
> — *The Secret Doctrine* 2:281

Nature is cyclical throughout: at one time fertile in spiritual things, at another barren. At this long-ago period of the third root-race, on the great continent of Lemuria,* now submerged, the cycle was against spiritual progress. A great downward sweep was in force, when expansion of physical and material energies were accelerated with the consequent retardation and contraction of spiritual power. The humanities of that period were part of the general evolutionary current, and individuals reacted to the coarsening atmosphere according to their nature. Some resisted its downward influence through awakened spirituality; others, weaker in understanding, vacillated between spirit and matter, between good and evil: sometimes listening to the promptings of intuition, at other times submerged by the rushing waves of the downward current. Still others, in whom the spark of intellectual splendor burned low, plunged headlong downstream, unmindful of the turbulent and muddy waters.

As the downward cycle proceeded, knowledge of spiritual verities and living of the life in accordance

---

*The name given in the 1850s by P. L. Sclater to a landmass which he showed, on zoological grounds, to have once extended from Africa to Australia (cf. *SD* 2:7). See Ignatius Donnelly, *Atlantis: The Antediluvian World*, p. 32, and Alfred Russel Wallace, *The Geographical Distribution of Animals*, Part I, ch. 4, pp. 76–7.

with them became a dull and useless tool in human hearts and minds. Such folly was inevitable in the course of cosmic events, and all things were provided for. Just as there are many types of people — some spiritual, others material, some highly intelligent, others slow of thought — so are there various grades of beings throughout the universe, ranging from the mineral, through the vegetable, animal, and human kingdom, and beyond to the head and hierarch of our earth.

During these first millennia the spiritual head and guardian of the earth had been stimulating wherever possible the individual fires of active spirituality. Gradually as knowledge of divine things became abused by those strong in will but weak in morality, truth was increasingly veiled. The planetary watcher now felt the need of selecting a band of co-workers to act as bodyguard and protector of the ancient wisdom. Alone a handful of spiritually illumined human beings, in whom the divine fervor burned bright, acknowledged wholehearted allegiance to their planetary mentor — the spiritual hierarch of humanity. Through long ages certain individuals had been watched over and guided, strengthened and tested in innumerable ways, and those who passed the test of self-knowledge and self-sacrifice were gathered together to form the first association of spiritual-divine human beings — the Great Brotherhood. As G. de Purucker elaborates:

> Then was formed or established or set in operation the gathering together of the very highest representatives, spiritually and intellectually speaking, that the human race as yet had given manifestation to; . . .
>
> . . . the Silent Watcher of the Globe, through the spiritual-magnetic attraction of like to like, was enabled to attract to the Path of Light, even from the earliest times of the Third Root-Race, certain unusual human individuals, early forerunners of the general Mānasaputric "descent," and thus to form with these individuals a Focus of Spiritual and Intellectual Light on Earth, this fact signifying not so much an association or society or brotherhood as a unity of human spiritual and intellectual Flames, so to speak, which then represented on Earth the heart of the Hierarchy of Compassion. . . .
>
> Now it was just this original focus of Living Flames, which never degenerated nor lost its high status of the mystic center on Earth through which poured the supernal glory of the Hierarchy of Compassion, today represented by the Great Brotherhood of the Mahātmans, . . . Thus it is that the Great Brotherhood traces an unbroken and uninterrupted

ancestry back to the original focus of Light of the Third Root-Race.

> — *The Esoteric Tradition* 2:1048-9n

Hence the elder brothers of the race remain "the elect custodians of the Mysteries revealed to mankind by the divine Teachers . . . and tradition whispers, what the secret teachings affirm, namely, that these Elect were the germ of a Hierarchy *which never died since that period*" (*SD* 2:281) — since the foundation and establishment of the Great Brotherhood some 12 million years ago. From this center for millions of years have been streaming in continuous procession rays of light and strength into the world at large and, more specifically, into the hearts of those whose lives are dedicated to the service of truth. From this Fraternity have gone forth messengers, masters of wisdom, to inspire the grand religions of the past, and they will continue to send forth their envoys as long as mankind requires their care.

Chapter 2

The First Mystery Schools

TIME MARCHED ON and the race waxed lusty in power. As Lemuria gave birth to Atlantis, the third root-race to the fourth, the fiercest battle was waged: the war between the lords of light and truth and the lords of darkness and ignorance.

Moral strength is not guaranteed by awakening intellect nor by the possession of psychic and physical power. The Atlanteans at their acme of development were a civilization of vigorous intellect motivated by psychophysical force, unreined in the main by moral stamina. Magic, which had been a natural gift of the Lemurians, in the hands of these giants became matter-magic, psychical magic, and the race plunged into an orgy of sorcery, the effects of which we are experiencing even today in outbursts of hate and madness.

Not all the Atlanteans, however, were overpowered by their own strength; not by any means. Nevertheless, a great portion of them became sorcerers of evil and perished in their tracks. Others, in whom the light of spirituality was "seen as through a glass darkly," became unhappy victims of the nefarious waves of unmoral power that swept over the continental system of Atlantis; in their confusion they wandered hither and yon, following false gods, unworthy guidance. A few — probably several millions, but few in proportion to the enormous population of the Atlantean continents — remained strong and clean throughout, morally illumined through contact with spirit. These became the chosen disciples of the Brotherhood, the stimulators of virtue and discipline in the land.

Until then there had been no call for Mysteries, truth having been the common property of mankind. With the increase of egoity,

> selfishness was born out of desires and passions hitherto unknown, and but too often knowledge and power were abused, until finally it became necessary to limit the number of those *who knew.* Thus arose Initiation.
>
> — "The Origin of the Mysteries," *BCW* 14:249

To insure the continuity of the race, something had to be done. Matters had come to such a pass that the only recourse was to establish a spiritual center in

each national unit which would serve as a safeguard
for the truths imparted there and as a secret training
center where genuine seekers could be disciplined and
instructed and, if found worthy, could learn truth
firsthand — i.e., through initiation.

The Brotherhood, therefore, which had already established invisible lines of esoteric instruction even in
late Lemurian times, in which those sensitive enough
could be trained, purified, and made strong for the
reception of truth and its safeguarding, now launched
a systematic campaign. Disciples, messengers, went
forth and inaugurated esoteric colleges, universities of
the soul, special training centers for the select purpose
of gathering into them the choicest men and women
for discipline and instruction in the mysteries of
nature.

Thus were established some four or five million
years ago, when Atlantis was threatening to destroy
itself through spiritual iniquity, the first Mystery
schools. From these early centers sprang other Mystery schools in all parts of the Atlantean world. By
the time the Atlanteans were in their heyday of *material* splendor, these schools were working their hardest
to stem the increasing tide of sorcery. Many —
millions probably — were saved through the establishment of the Mysteries. The more awakened of the

race intuitively sought training there, while the great bulk of humanity, though unable to partake of the sacred rites of initiation on account of insufficient interior development, nevertheless were helped by the indirect radiation of spiritual force.

There were those, however, who had tasted of evil and found it to their liking, and whose hardening hearts led them to receive instruction in evil discipline. Simultaneously, therefore, with the establishment of spiritual centers of light and truth, schools of evil were founded whose pledged votaries became in time the left-hand adepts. The lords of light and truth united in a calm invincible force to

> resist the terrible and ever-growing iniquities of the left-hand Adepts, the Atlanteans. This led to the foundation of still more Secret Schools, temples of learning, and of Mysteries inaccessible to all except after the most terrible trials and probations. . . .
>
> . . . The Mysteries were imparted to the elect of that Race when the average Atlantean had begun to fall too deeply into sin to be trusted with the secrets of Nature. — Ibid. 14:251, 246

There now occurred the most dramatic moment — a moment millions of years long — in the whole history of this round: the turning point of the cycle from matter to spirit. At the middle of the fourth root-race in this fourth round the Atlanteans saw spirit and matter equilibrated: *which way would the scales turn?* Towards light and spirit, and the eventual liberation of mankind? Towards darkness and matter, and the enslavement of humanity? A great tremor shook the earth: would innate spirituality prove stronger than the weight of acquired materiality? Would mankind ascend the luminous arc or fall headlong into the pit of matter on the descending shadowy arc? Of the billions of human beings whose hearts must be weighed against the feather of spirit, each one had to pass the fateful test alone: failure, and be swept downwards into still greater materiality, unable to rise with spirit during the present great world cycle; success, and the rise upwards in the general current of evolutionary progress until self-conscious oneness with divinity may again be reclaimed.

The moment of a million years or so passed. Fortunately for the human race, due in large part to the efforts of the Mystery schools, the majority retained sufficient awareness of divinity to balance the scales in their favor. An unconscious choice for millions, but nevertheless a choice made by the better part of their natures — by what slender majority perhaps we shall never know.

Chapter 3

Raison d'être of the Mysteries

CATACLYSM AFTER CATACLYSM occurred, and the leaden slag of the fourth race sank to its doom, deluged by the waters of heaven and earth as they flooded the lands according to karmic law. Along with the sinking of Atlantis, which extended over several million years, new lands had been rising in other parts of the globe, and these became peopled as time went by with certain of the Atlanteans who settled there in two or three great migratory waves (see G. de Purucker, *Studies in Occult Philosophy*, pp. 16–25).

Thus the fourth root-race gave birth to the fifth whose cradleland was the Desert of Shamo or Gobi and surrounding tablelands — a country whose present sandy wastes give no hint of lands once rich with verdure, where forests and lakes witnessed a succession of civilizations as grand as any the world has ever known. Here for many millions of years, while Atlantis was involved in her death struggle, seeds of the new race were being sown in virgin soil.

Nature is beneficent in her workings. While the consequences of her human children must be met and faced by them through the working of karma and cyclic reimbodiment, yet at each new racial birth she casts her seed in freshly-turned soil, so that the child-race may be conceived in purity and nurtured in spirituality. Peopled thus with egos who had remained clean and strong through the Atlantean upheavals, and helped once again by the reentrance into their midst of semi-divine beings, the new race became a focus of spiritual light. As the Master KH wrote:

> the *highest* Planetary Spirits, those, who can no longer err . . . appear on Earth but at the origin of every *new* human kind; at the junction of, and close of the two ends of the great cycle. And, they remain with man no longer than the time required for the eternal truths they teach to impress themselves so forcibly upon the plastic minds of the new races as to warrant them from being lost or entirely forgotten in ages hereafter, by the forthcoming generations. The mission of the planetary Spirit is but to strike the KEY NOTE OF TRUTH.
> — *The Mahatma Letters to A. P. Sinnett,*
> Letter IX, pp. 40–1

Simultaneously with the establishment of the Mystery schools in Atlantis some four or five million years ago, the fifth or Aryan race* was slowly coming into being, immensely aided by egos of spiritual refinement attracted there by ties of divine kinship. Gradually the soil was prepared and, the work of striking the "Keynote of Truth" having been accomplished, the demigods retired to their superior spheres. One million years ago the new race was ushered into adult existence impressed with the knowledge of "eternal truths."

As the centuries passed and civilization succeeded civilization, the love of truth once again became dimmed in human hearts and the ancient precepts fell into disuse. The Mysteries were withdrawn even further, so that the knowledge once universal became the prized guerdon bestowed by the great Brotherhood upon that choice minority whose lives were dedicated to truth and truth alone, unstained by weakness or selfish ambition. With enduring consistency the ongoing purpose of the

---

**Aryan* is derived from the Sanskrit *ārya,* "noble," and originally referred to the Indo-European peoples who migrated out of Central Asia to Europe, the Mediterranean basin, Persia, and the Indian peninsula. In theosophic usage, the Aryan or fifth race more generally denotes the present human evolutionary cycle which comprises, like the fourth race, "almost a countless number of races and nations" (*SD* 2:433–4 & nn).

Mysteries has remained threefold in character:

(1) the persistent spiritualization of the thought-life of humanity so that knowledge of things spiritual may penetrate into the heart, and life in time may become a benediction of peace instead of a tragedy of conflict;

(2) seeding grounds of adepts, nurseries for future recruits, who through trial and initiation may become fit to receive the supreme dignity of membership in the great Brotherhood; and

(3) the preservation of truth for future races unsullied by human hand; and the polishing of the knowledge of truth through investigation by trained seers of the secrets of nature in worlds visible and invisible.

The first of these aims is fulfilled by the periodic appearance of world teachers, the inspirers of what later became the great religious and philosophical schools: messengers from the Lodge who come forth at cyclic periods to strike anew the "Keynote of Truth." Hence every great religion, every noble philosophy, every fundamental scientific insight was born from the Sanctuary, to become a *new* religion, a *new* philosophy, a *new* science: fresh and new for the age and the people, but ancient beyond time because nurtured in the womb of esoteric antiquity.

> All that is good, noble, and grand in human nature, every divine faculty and aspiration, were cultured by the Priest-Philosophers who sought to develop them in their Initiates. Their code of ethics, based on altruism, has become universal.
> — "The Origin of the Mysteries," *BCW* 14:256

The second of these aims is ages-long in accomplishment and deeply occult: to rouse the hidden fire of divinity in the human soul, and through the kindling of that flame burn the dross of imperfection, sloth, and unworthy desire from the heart. One of the impelling aims of such discipline is to restore to humanity *inner* sight, to free people "from every danger of being enslaved whether by a man or an idea" (*BCW* 14:251; see also *ML*, pp. 40–1).

The disciple must become *vajradhara* ("diamond-bearer"), a title used for Bodhisattva Gautama, whose many-faceted heart was ever merciful in reflecting human sorrow, but whose spiritual essence was like a diamond, unyielding at its core to the subtle disguise of illusion (māyā).

The third of these aims is made possible through the selection of new recruits into the Brotherhood, so that (a) truth may be preserved untarnished by human selfishness; and (b) investigation into the arcana of nature may go on unhindered, and the results of such examination by generations of trained seers be checked and rechecked, and only then recorded as occult fact for the benefit of humanity.

As far as the labor of the Masters is concerned, the following written by one of their number in 1881 speaks for itself:

> If, for generations we have "shut out the world from the Knowledge of our Knowledge," it is on account of its absolute unfitness; and if, notwithstanding proofs given, it still refuses yielding to evidence, then will we at the End of this cycle retire into solitude and our kingdom of silence once more. . . . We have offered to exhume the primeval strata of man's being, his basic nature, and lay bare the wonderful complications of his inner Self — something never to be achieved by physiology or even psychology in its ultimate expression — and demonstrate it scientifically. It matters not to them, if the excavations be so deep, the rocks so rough and sharp, that in diving into that, to them, fathomless ocean, most of us perish in the dangerous exploration; for it is we who were the divers and the pioneers and the men of science have but to reap where we have sown. It is our mission to plunge and bring the pearls of Truth to the surface; theirs — to clean and set them

into scientific jewels. And, if they refuse to touch the ill-shapen, oyster-shell, insisting that there is, nor *cannot* be any precious pearl inside it, then shall we once more wash our hands of any responsibility before human-kind. — *ML*, pp. 50–1

Unthanked, unknown, unconsidered, the Masters go on in their compassionate work for mankind's enlightenment, a work that has never ceased in its outpouring of spiritual vitality for many millions of years, to continue another such period if necessity demand, until such time as humanity stirs from its lethargy and once again wills to unite its heart with truth. Master KH continues:

For countless generations hath the adept builded a fane of imperishable rocks, a giant's Tower of INFINITE THOUGHT, wherein the Titan dwelt, and will yet, if need be, dwell alone, emerging from it but at the end of every cycle, to invite the elect of mankind to cooperate with him and help in his turn enlighten superstitious man. And we will go on in that periodical work of ours; we will not allow ourselves to be baffled in our philanthropic attempts until that day when the foundations of a new continent of thought are so firmly built that no amount of opposition and ignorant malice guided by the Brethren of the Shadow will be found to prevail. — p. 51

Chapter 4

The Pattern of Esotericism

> To the spiritual eagle eye of the seer and the prophet of
> every race, Ariadne's thread stretches beyond that "his-
> toric period" without break or flaw, surely and steadily,
> into the very night of time; and the hand which holds
> it is too mighty to drop it, or even let it break.
>
> — *The Secret Doctrine* 2:67

THIS THREAD OF ESOTERICISM stretches further still
into the dawntime of the human race, where
"Truth, high-seated upon its rock of adamant, is alone
eternal and supreme" (*Isis Unveiled* 1:v). Where is
this truth, this loom of esoteric history, and what the
pattern of its fabric? In the home of the Brotherhood
stands this loom, whose warp is the ancient threads of
initiation held in occult tension by the sacrifice of
adepts, and whose woof is woven century by century
as each national unit spins the luminous threads of
esotericism in its Mystery centers.

Profane history reveals scarcely anything of consecutive value, except insofar as the relics of this mystic pageantry all point to an identic motif. To "have a consecutive and full history of *our* race from its incipient stage down to the present times," archaic records must needs be sought. By such alone could one trace even in faint outline the ancient pattern. Access to these, however, is the privilege of the adept alone, for such "knowledge is only for the *highest* Initiates, who do not take their students into their confidence" (*SD* 2:437–8). Nevertheless, we have received a priceless gift: the benefit of evidence gathered by those who have penetrated the veils of the adyta and have had the compassion to return and share with us a guarded portion of their vision. Study of their findings may at first reveal only a broken pattern, but if faithfully pursued such study will point with unmistakable clarity to one universal source of truth.

From Central Asia whose lands comprised a vast territory, including the Desert of Gobi or Shamo, the mountains of Tien Shan and Kuen Lun, the regions of Baluchistan, Afghanistan, Persia, and Turkestan, went forth bands of emigrants, in large part glowing with determination to conquer, to subdue, and many were the battles waged in those early days. A primal cause, yet unrecognized by the populace, was the urge of the Brotherhood aided by karma to carry the light of the

Mysteries into other lands, to spread the ancient wisdom far and wide on the surface of the earth:

> Not one people alone inhabited and built up these civilizations of Central Asia. They were recurrent waves of our present Fifth Root-Race. . . . each one of such civilizations being in its turn a cradle out of which grew children-colonies sent forth to carry light and initiation to what were then barbarous and uncultivated parts of the world, such as what is now Europe, what is now China, what is now Siberia, what is now India.   — *SOP*, pp. 23, 22

To Bhārata-varsha or India went forth the Āryas or "worthy ones," a band of emigrants who founded a civilization and a culture as yet unrivaled in esoteric history, whose ramifications of spiritual influence extended to Egypt, Asia Minor, and Europe. Another band moved westward to Egypt, the "gift of the Nile" as Herodotus called it, and mixing with the aboriginal stock peopled its valleys. From this union sprang a princely civilization, the glory of which remains after thousands of centuries, the more so as the influence of its Mysteries spread far and wide as conquering nation after conquering nation became captive to the interior grandeur of Egypt. Persia, Babylonia, Judea and Crete, Greece and Rome, all trace their spiritual inspiration to the Egyptian and early Aryan cultures. Furthermore, so immense in esoteric power were these primeval civilizations, that

> there are records which show Egyptian priests — Initiates — journeying in a North-Westerly direction, *by land, viâ* what became later the Straits of Gibraltar; turning North and travelling through the future Phoenician settlements of Southern Gaul; then still further North, until reaching Carnac (Morbihan) they turned to the West again and arrived, *still travelling by land,* on the North-Western promontory of the New Continent [the British Isles].
>
> What was the object of their long journey? And how far back must we place the date of such visits? The archaic records show the Initiates of the Second Sub-race of the Aryan family moving from one land to the other for the purpose of supervising the building of *menhirs* and dolmens, of colossal Zodiacs in stone, and places of sepulchre to serve as receptacles for the ashes of generations to come.   — *SD* 2:750

What was the mainspring of these civilizations but the Mystery-teachings — teachings which penetrated into the very thought-life of nations, perhaps unknown of source, unrecognized by the multitudes as esoteric? Nonetheless they constituted the inspiration of the artist in his search for divinity, the intuition of the poet in his yearning for truth, and the resounding harmony of the musician as he sought the music of the spheres. It is no idle phrase to say that all things of spiritual, intellectual, and artistic value were born root and seed from the Sanctuary.

What are the stone and papyrus of Egypt but witness to knowledge of ancient truths long forgotten? The scenes of the weighing of the heart against the feather of truth in the papyri of *Pert Em Hru* — "Coming forth into Day," commonly known as the *Book of the Dead* — portray in symbol and allegory what actually took place in the secret chambers of the initiation-pyramids. Living testimonial is the Great Pyramid of Khufu or Cheops, which H. P. Blavatsky hints more than once may go back at least 75,000 years BC, if not more (see *SD* 2:432, 750).

What of the Druids and their ancient ceremonies under oak and myrtle, with their stone monuments so oriented that the beams of the rising sun touched the brow of the candidate as he rose from his couch of initiation "clothed with the sun," literally aflame with solar glory? Whence the training of their candidates in three degrees, a training which demanded absolute moral purity, spiritual vigor, and profound under-standing of truth?

What about Persia and its long line of Zoroasters, within whose mystic seven-chambered centers truths of great intellectual and spiritual value were taught to neophytes who underwent the traditional discipline of the Mysteries? Were the Magi born from any other source than the archaic mother of occultism? What of the Orphic Mysteries, whose austere discipline and esoteric content may have had a stronger impact on Greek culture than the Eleusinian Mysteries, so popular for centuries? Do not the teachings of Orpheus indicate an Eastern origin reminiscent of those from India's *āśramas* or mystery-temples? Did not Pythagoras and Plato likewise travel India-wards and bring back to their disciples the identic pattern of esotericism?

Thus one might go on, with the Norse and Germanic mysticism, the Hindu and Chinese philosophies, the Greek and Roman ceremonial — all weavers of one pattern in one universal motif, a motif applicable to all times, to all nations, because capable of infinite variations. To grasp the *inner* purport of one Mystery school is to perceive the sacred identity of all of them — not in detail of cultural and ethnic interpretation, but in esoteric essentials.

What therefore is the test of truth? One basic requirement is universality: has it been taught by all those who have been "clothed with the central sun" of initiation? Did Buddha Gautama instruct his disciples in the selfsame doctrine that Christ Jesus did? Did Śankarāchārya teach the same esotericism that Pythagoras and Empedocles did? Were Zoroaster and Tsong-kha-pa born in their adepthood from the same womb of the initiation chamber as Apollonius of Tyana, Orpheus, or Lao-Tzŭ? Have Persia and Greece, China and ancient America, Iceland, Wales, and Babylonia all received a message which, stripped of outer vestments, is one in essentials? Assuredly, it is so, for such patterns have been woven on one loom — the ageless loom of truth.

These Mystery schools are not a unique system but, based on the spiritual structure of the universe, they were

> established from the same motives of compassion that presided over the acts of the great actors of the primal drama, the opening acts of our manvantara. They copied, as it were in miniature, what took place in those primordial times, and what took place in actual life in the Hierarchy of Compassion on our earth, or that section, rather, of the Hierarchy of Compassion which we call the Great White Lodge.
>
> — G. de Purucker, *Fundamentals of the Esoteric Philosophy*, 2nd ed., p. 322

One primeval humanity, many children-colonies; one Mystery teaching, many Mystery schools; one archaic pattern, many variations of color and texture as each nation contributes the woof of its national Mysteries. Three are the variants of motif as seen from the present:

(1) the original unveiling of truth to infant humanity by divine instructors working in consonance with the spiritual planetary of our earth who, through the early millennia, successfully gathered together the choice few into a center of esoteric light — the great Brotherhood;

(2) the secondary unveiling springing directly as the fruit of the first: the spiritualizing influences uninterruptedly sent forth by the Brotherhood, and more specifically energized at cyclic intervals by their disciples, the great world teachers; and

(3) the third unveiling born as the progeny of (1) and (2): the penetration of truth into human life through the Mystery schools, the centers of esoteric discipline, in whose inner chambers initiation of the "elect" alone takes place, but in whose outer courts the world-at-large may seek entrance to learn fundamental verities so that life may be ennobled and death accepted as naturally as is sleep. Thus is the pattern of esotericism woven century by century on the loom of truth.

Chapter 5

Dual Character of the Mysteries

> The whole essence of truth *cannot be transmitted from mouth to ear.* Nor can any pen describe it, not even that of the recording Angel, unless man finds the answer in the sanctuary of his own heart, in the innermost depths of his divine intuitions.
>
> — *The Secret Doctrine* 2:516

HOW ARE THOSE "innermost depths" to be sounded, so that knowledge of reality may be won? Through training, discipline, and self-born wisdom. Such training and soul-discipline is the distinguishing mark of the Mystery colleges, which since their inauguration have been divided into two parts: the exoteric form commonly known as the Lesser Mysteries, open to all sincere and honorable candidates for deeper learning; and the esoteric form, or the Greater Mysteries, whose doors open but to the few and whose initiation into adeptship is the reward of those whose interior nobility enables them to undergo the solar rite (see chapters 8 and 9).

Universal testimony of stone and papyrus, symbol and allegory, cave and crypt, tells of the twofold trial of neophytes. Jesus the Avatāra spoke to the multitudes in parable, but "when they were alone, he expounded all things to his disciples" (*Mark* 4:34). The Essenes had their greater and minor Mysteries, in the former of which Jesus of Nazareth is believed to have been initiated.

The Chinese Buddhists hold to a well-loved tradition that Buddha Gautama had two doctrines: one for the people and his lay-disciples; the other for his arhats. His invariable principle was

> to refuse no one admission into the ranks of candidates for Arhatship, but never to divulge the final mysteries except to those who had proved themselves, during long years of probation, to be worthy of Initiation.
> — "The Doctrine of Avatāras," *BCW* 14:370

Intensity of purpose marks the Hebrew initiates in their shrouding of inner teaching. To the multitude they taught the Tōrāh, the "Law," but to the few they taught its unwritten interpretation, the "Secret Wisdom" — *ḥokhmāh nistorāh* — "in 'darkness, in a deserted place, and after many and terrific trials.' . . . Delivered *only as a mystery*, it was communicated to the candidate orally, *'face to face and mouth to ear.'*"

The Persian and Chaldean Magi also were of two castes: "the initiated and those who were allowed to officiate in the popular rites only" (see *Isis* 2:306n and *The Kabbalah* by Christian D. Ginsburg, p. 86).

Eleusis and Samothrace are limned in exquisite silhouette against the blue-black sky of history. Classical scholars tell us that the Lesser Mysteries were conducted in the springtime at Agrai near Athens, while the Greater Mysteries were celebrated in the autumn at Eleusis. In the Lesser Mysteries the candidates who experienced the first rites were called *mystai* (the closed of eye and mouth). In the Greater Mysteries the mystai became *epoptai* (the clear-seeing), who participated in the mysteries of the Divine Elysion — i.e., communion with the divine.

Similarly, the Hindu arhat, the Scandinavian skald, and the Welsh bard guarded the soul of esotericism with the sanctity of their lives and the discipline of their sacred tradition:

> Belonging to every temple there were attached the "hierophants" of the *inner* sanctuary, and the secular clergy who were not even instructed in the Mysteries.
>
> — *Isis* 2:306n

Further, in all ancient countries "every *great* temple had its private or secret Mystery-School which was unknown to the multitude or partially known," and which was attached to it as a secret body. A Mystery school is not necessarily a school of people situated at some specific place, with definite and fixed locality throughout time, and with physical conditions of environment always alike. Wherever the need is great, work must be done; and the "mistake of all scholars and mystics is to put too much emphasis upon *places* as Mystery-Schools" (*SOP*, pp. 635, 634).

What about the temples of Greece and Rome, of Syria and Judea; the cave-temples of Elephanta and Karli in India; the dagobas of Buddhist countries; the pyramids of Egypt and Peru, Mexico and Yucatán? What of Stonehenge in England; Carnac in Brittany; Sippara in Assyria; Babylon, Borsippa and Erech in Babylonia; Ecbatana in Media; Bibracte in Gaul; and last but not least, Iona in Scotland whose secret learning was as a jewel of wisdom set in the heart of the northern land? Where are they now? Mere names, relics, remnants of forgotten splendor — or so it would appear.

A Mystery school is not dependent on location; rather it is an association or brotherhood of spiritually disciplined individuals bound by one common purpose, service to humanity, a service intelligently and compassionately rendered because born of love and wisdom. It is a fact, nevertheless, that certain centers appear to be more favorable to success in spiritual things than others. Why, for instance, were the ancient seats of the Mysteries almost invariably in rock-temple or subterranean cave, in forest or mountain pass, in pyramid chamber or temple crypt? Because the currents of the astral light become quieter, more peaceful, cleaner, the farther removed from the madding crowd. Rarely will one find a seat of esoteric training near a large metropolis, for such are "swirling whirlpools . . . ganglia, nerve-centers, in the lower regions of the Astral Light" (*ET* 2:1026).

Hence the locations of the Greater Mysteries were usually carefully chosen and their schools were those which paid no attention to buildings of any kind, mainly for the reason that buildings would at once attract attention and draw public notice, which is the very thing that these more secret, more esoteric Schools tried to avoid. Thus sometimes, when the temples were mere seats of exoteric ritual, the Mystery-Schools were held apart in secret, conducting their gatherings, meetings, initiations, initiatory rites, usually in caves carefully prepared and hid from common knowledge, occasionally even under the open sky as the Druids did among the oaks in their semi-primeval forests in Britain and in Brittany; and even in a few cases having no permanent or set location; but the Initiates receiving word where to meet from time to time, and to carry on their initiatory functions.

— *SOP*, p. 635

It is the places of quiet, of peace, of strong silence, where the Adepts find themselves drawn, and where the secret or Greater Mysteries can most effectively function. There in the recesses of their initiation chambers the forces and currents are those of the higher astral light, the ākāśa, the tenuous substance which responds to the higher currents of spirit and intellect. In this way does the Brotherhood transmit its potent spiritual vitality to the initiation halls, and the candidate whose seven-rayed soul is attuned may receive the divine imprint.

Chapter 6

Degrees of Initiation

EVERY COUNTRY HAS ITS own methods of preserving the knowledge and tradition of the Mysteries. The degrees are variously reckoned, sometimes four, five, seven, or even ten; but whatever the divisions, during the days of their purity they all honored the one divine purpose of consummating the spiritual marriage of the higher self with the awakened human soul, from which union springs the seer, the adept, the master of life. Through the ravages of time and priestcraft, and the tangle of intrigue and ignorance in which exoteric rites are enmeshed, one perceives the venerable tradition.

In Asia Minor, Theon of Smyrna writes of five degrees in the initiatory cycle: (1) "the preliminary purification," because taking part in the Mysteries "must not be indiscriminately given to all who desire it"; (2) "the tradition of sacred things" which constitutes the "initiation proper"; (3) the "epoptic revelation," where the candidate may experience direct intuition of truth; (4) "the binding of the head and placement of the crown" — a clear reference to the mystical authority received with the crown of initiation to pass on the sacred tradition to others; and, finally, (5) "friendship and interior communion" with divinity — this was considered the highest and most solemn mystery of all, the complete assimilation of the enlightened mind with the divine self (see Theon of Smyrna, *Mathematics Useful for Understanding Plato*, pp. 8–9; also *Isis* 1:xiv–xv, 2:101).

In Persia during the time of Mithraism, when the sun god was honored above earthly things, seven were the degrees, the candidate receiving a name relevant to each stage of interior growth. Using the Graeco-Latin names that have come down to us, the first-degree neophyte was called *Corax*, "raven" — the dark bird, one in whom the light of wisdom had not yet awakened in great measure. It signified likewise a servant: one who gives of his heart totally before receiving admission into the second degree which was termed *Cryphius*, "occult": one accepted as a disciple of esoteric lore; the third was *Miles*, "soldier," one who had received sufficient training and purification to become a worker for good. The fourth — *Leo*, "lion," emblem of solar power — has reference to the fourth initiation in which the candidate begins the conscious solarizing of the nature through instruction and specialized training (see chapters 7 and 8). The fifth degree was known as *Perses*, "Persian," signifying to the Persians of the time one who was becoming spiritually human — mānasaputrized, that is, mind-born. The sixth, *Heliodromus*, "messenger or runner of Helios (the sun)" is a reference to Mercury or Budha, as messenger between the sun in the cosmos and the sun in man: the bloom of buddhi. The final and seventh was called *Pater*, "father," the state of a Full Initiate (see *The Ancient Mysteries, A Sourcebook*, Marvin W. Meyer, editor, pp. 200–1; also *ET* 2:864).

The Hindus likewise had various names for their disciples as they passed from one degree to another. For instance, in one school the candidates received the names of the ten avatāras of Vishnu. The first degree neophyte was termed *Matsya*, "fish": one yet low in the scale of spiritual mastery. The second was *Kūrma*, "tortoise": one step higher in evolutionary development. The third degree was called *Varāha*, "boar," a further advance in individualization, while the fourth was termed *Nara-simha*, "man-lion." This fourth stage marks the turning point between the preliminary degrees of the Lesser Mysteries and the advanced degrees of the Greater Mysteries. This title of man-lion points to the choice demanded of the aspirant between dominance of animal soul qualities and the supremacy henceforth of the truly human attributes. Success in the fourth degree insured the entrance into the fifth called *Vāmana,* "dwarf," in which the candidate assumed the robes of occult humanhood, though such humanhood was as yet infantile compared to full mastery. *Paraśu-Rāma,* "Rāma with an axe," name of the sixth-degree neophyte, suggests one capable of hewing his way with equanimity through the worlds of both spirit and matter. In the seventh degree the disciple becomes fully humanized, receiving the name of Rāma, hero of the *Rāmāyana,* an important epic of Hindustan.

The last three degrees, the eighth, ninth, and tenth, are called respectively: *Krishna,* the avatāra whose death ushered in the Kali yuga some 5,000 years ago; *Buddha,* whose renunciation of nirvana brought light and peace to a sorrowing world; and the final and tenth, *Kalkin* or Kalkī, the "white-horse" avatāra who is yet to come. As noted in the *Vishnu Purāna* (Bk IV, ch. xxiv), he is destined to appear at the end of the Kali or Iron Age, seated on a white horse, with a drawn sword blazing like a comet, for the destruction of the wicked, the renovation of creation, and the restoration of purity. In ancient symbology the horse also symbolized the sun, hence the tenth avatāra will come riding the steed of solar glory to usher in the New Age clothed with the sun of spiritual illumination.*

While seven were the degrees usually enumerated in the Mysteries, hints have been given of three higher degrees than the seventh. But so esoteric would these be that only the most spiritualized of humanity could comprehend and hence undertake these divine initiations.

Rare indeed are those who become avatāra-like; rarer still, "as rare as are the flowers of the Udumbara-tree" are the Buddhas. As for the tenth and last — such has been left unmarred by description.

*See John Dowson, *A Classical Dictionary of Hindu Mythology and Religion, Geography, History, and Literature,* 6th ed., p. 38; also H. P. Blavatsky, *Theosophical Glossary,* p. 170.

Chapter 7

The Lesser Mysteries

THE LESSER MYSTERIES are a preparation of the neophyte for initiation in the Greater Mysteries through various degrees of purification and discipline combined with training in intellectual and spiritual perception. As indicated in the previous chapter, seven were the degrees usually reckoned, the first three comprising the Lesser Mysteries. The fourth degree is the turning or deciding point where those who underwent the discipline and training of the preliminary stages are put to the test of actual experience in self-identification. If the candidate pass this fourth trial successfully, he enters upon more stringent discipline and purification, and a more intimate relationship between teacher and pupil. Henceforth he is a pledged disciple, his will is set firmly to pass successfully the fifth, sixth, and seventh degrees which comprise the Greater Mysteries.

The trials of the Lesser Mysteries are comparatively simple, but as the disciple proves his earnestness and ability to stand the probationary tests, the training becomes more rigorous, the demands upon his nature more severe, and the hand of karma deals more sternly with error.

Two particular features mark the Minor Mysteries: (a) instruction in the deeper sciences of the cosmos; and (b) dramatic rites portraying that which the initiant must go through without outside help in the Greater Mysteries. In the Eleusinian Mysteries, for example, the sacred rites acted as a spiritual aid in stimulating the candidate to live the higher life, as well as familiarizing him with the routes of the initiatory process.

To witness or participate in a drama is quite different from suffering the actual experience; even so, this serves as preliminary fortification to the neophyte when the time comes for the greater initiations. The Lesser Mysteries have been known and recognized by the keenest minds of all ages as institutions of higher learning for those who had proved themselves worthy and fit.

From the Mystery schools, knowledge of truth permeates the mental strata of the surrounding country, as initiates in the preliminary degrees mingle with the world. In Greece and Rome, nearly all the great men of historic note were initiates of one or more degrees of the Lesser Mysteries. This did not pertain to murderers or conquerors by the sword, for almost universally these were not initiates of the Mysteries, although in the declining days of the Roman Empire many applicants of indifferent caliber underwent the introductory rites in a more or less perfunctory fashion.

In fact, the Mysteries in olden times were regarded so highly that preparation for entrance was deemed the most royal gift a father could bequeath his sons. At the age of seven years, boys were received and disciplined in heart and mind, so that on reaching adulthood they either took their places in the world and exerted an edifying influence among the people; or if they were especially favored by right of inner fitness, they remained within the Sanctuary and passed as far as they could into the Greater Mysteries. Certain ones were trained for the sole purpose of teaching the laws of life in seats of higher learning; others received the preliminary rites in order to prepare them to govern the State with equanimity and honor. Still others underwent the discipline and purification of the first degrees and then devoted their lives to bringing beauty to mankind, whether in sculpture or color, in verse or harmony. Thus did these early civilizations ripen in spiritual things under the guidance of initiated philosophers and statesmen, artists, and musicians.

Many branches of the arts and sciences were taught in the Lesser Mysteries, notably geography, astronomy, chemistry, physiology, psychology, geology, meteorology, as well as music, the "most divine and *spiritual* of arts" (*ML*, Letter xxivb, p. 188); similarly art and architecture were studied, whose lost "canon of proportion" immortalized the Greek temples. These sciences were held as secret studies of the Mysteries, not because they would not have been understood if taught as schools and universities teach them today, but because such sciences and arts were studied from their *causal* rather than their effectual aspect.

Much derision has been cast on the ancients for withholding knowledge that even a child can understand in its simpler forms. Certainly the simpler forms were taught openly, but their *occult* background was kept rigidly secret (as it is even now, though the world at large little dreams of this fact) as fit only for those who would not misuse the knowledge obtained. Can as much wisdom be shown today when, as soon as scientists discover some new device, opportunity is instantly found to turn that invention to destructive uses? One is driven to admire the strength and wisdom of the ancients who knew better than to turn knowledge over indiscriminately to those lacking moral control. With all our boasted superiority, we have not yet caught up on all lines with the scientific knowledge of our ancient forebears.

As H. P. Blavatsky wrote in 1877:

> If modern masters are so much in advance of the old ones, why do they not restore to us the lost arts of our postdiluvian forefathers? Why do they not give us the unfading colors of Luxor — the Tyrian purple; the bright vermilion and dazzling blue which decorate the walls of this place, and are as bright as on the first day of their application? The indestructible cement of the pyramids and of ancient aqueducts; the Damascus blade, which can be turned like a corkscrew in its scabbard without breaking; the gorgeous, unparalleled tints of the stained glass that is found amid the dust of old ruins and beams in the windows of ancient cathedrals; and the secret of the true malleable glass? And if chemistry is so little able to rival even with the early mediaeval ages in some arts, why boast of achievements which, according to strong probability, were perfectly known thousands of years ago? The more archaeology and philology advance, the more humiliating to our pride are the discoveries which are daily made, the more glorious testimony do they bear in behalf of those who, perhaps on account of the distance of their remote antiquity, have been until now considered ignorant flounderers in the deepest mire of superstition. — *Isis* 1:239

In the Mysteries, geography was not merely a study of topography; rather the periodical risings and sinkings of continents was the subject of investigation in accordance with the cyclic events of racial history; secret centers of the earth were learned of, and our intimate relation to the two poles and the four points of the compass. HPB suggestively hints:

> The two poles are called the right and left ends of our globe — the right being the North Pole — or the head and feet of the earth. Every beneficent (astral and cosmic) action comes from the North; every lethal influence from the South Pole. They are much connected with and influence *"right" and "left" hand magic.*   — *SD* 2:400n

Meteorology was the study of the currents of wind and rain, not from the effectual standpoint, but as bearing streams of vital energy from all parts of the solar system and beyond. Lightning and thunder, etc., were not merely electromagnetic phenomena — words that are accurate enough, yet unless occultly understood convey little more than a statement of effects produced. When considered from the causal aspect they are seen to be outer manifestations of interior forces bursting from cosmic space into our atmosphere and affecting the lives of earth.

In Chaldea, Egypt, Mexico and Peru, Wales, Iceland, and India, astrology was regarded with veneration. Its deeper teachings were transmitted from mouth to ear, so sacred and profoundly spiritual were they then considered. Mere fortune-telling and other similar trifles were held vulgar in the eyes of the hierophants. The recognized influences of the sun and planets upon human beings were not viewed as simply mechanical, compelling individuals to this or that character or mode of conduct. Such interchange of planetary and solar life energies among terrestrial beings was understood as springing from our common galactic heritage. The septenary nature of the planets was taken into account in reckoning septenary human nature. Hence the intermingling of life-atoms from the various planetary systems with the earth, and vice versa, constitutes one of the major studies of esoteric astrology.

Furthermore, the science of prediction of tremendous cyclic occurrences on earth was mastered not only in India to a fine hair's breadth (see the *Sūrya-Siddhānta* of Asuramaya, the oldest treatise on astronomy extant, *SD* 2:326), but also in ancient Chaldea, whose modern representatives of some four and five thousand years ago still held archaic astrology as a major characteristic of their secret Mysteries. The famous ziggurat or high tower of Borsippa in Babylonia is clear testimonial to knowledge of the sevenfold planetary influences on humanity. Called the stages of the seven spheres, each of its stories bore a different color, representative of one of the seven sacred planets. At the top of a ziggurat was a sacred shrine, often with a table or couch of gold.

Thus what may have seemed to the public mere astronomical observatories were secret training centers within whose inner recesses esoteric astrology formed one of the important studies of the Lesser Mysteries. Medicine and surgery, physics and alchemy, poetry, mathematics, and philosophy likewise were studied from their inner standpoint. This instruction consists not in the learning by rote of scores of formulae, but in the inner perception of occult rationale, so that knowledge benevolently applied for others may in time become wisdom.

However fascinating to the imagination and of whatever degree of intellectual and psychic stimulation to the neophyte were these studies, they were not the major aim of the Mysteries. Behind all training of the mind was the impelling urge for *soul purification* through discipline and contemplation. As stimulus and guidance, dramatic presentations were given of the descent of the candidate into the underworld, his trial in the nether regions through meeting and conquering himself, his ascent into the stream of life and light, culminating in final communion and "friendship" with the divinities. So effective were the dramatic rites that participation in them constituted a signal part of the initiatory training in preparation for the Greater Mysteries.

Comparison of the ritual of the Lesser Mysteries, as practiced in the ancient world with slight variations of detail, reveals the universal story of the descent into the underworld in the symbol of the wheat or corn deity. The seed or grain represents the candidate. As the seed enters into the dark regions of the moist earth, many are the difficulties of soil and environment to contend with; it "dies" in giving birth to root and stalk. Finally, as the period of germination expires, tender shoots of the grain sprout above the surface of the earth, and in time the seed-that-was bursts forth in flower with the aid of sun and rain. In like manner the candidate "dies" in the regions of the underworld, the lower spheres, where he meets and conquers the difficulties of environment; shedding his impermanent self, he dies in giving birth to budding masterhood. At the appropriate hour, the disciple-that-was rises to the spheres of light and life; taken into the presence of other plants of divinity, he finds friendship with the gods and blooms into the full flower of adepthood.

Thus is dramatized in esoteric imagery the spiritual travail of those *"giving birth to themselves"* (*SD* 2:559) — as an ancient manuscript describes the birth of the adept within the neophyte, the supreme initiation.

Chapter 8

The Greater Mysteries

THE GREATER MYSTERIES entered upon by the neophyte, after the successful consummation of the preliminary degrees, constitute the becoming by individual experience of that which had been learned in the Lesser Mysteries. In this higher department of esoteric training, no quarter is given. The neophyte must face himself and conquer — or die. All the stretches of his complex nature, from the divinely inspired to the grossly material, must be investigated and controlled. By this time the aspirant must have developed sufficient spiritual stamina to withstand reality. He must *become* nature in her lower and higher regions, pass the supreme test of self-identification, and yet retain his soul integrity.

Even as late as the second century, the rites of the Egyptian Mysteries, however modified by Greek influence, were carried on with due and appropriate reverence. Disciples from surrounding countries sought initiation there as a fitting advancement following their own ceremonies. Apuleius, Latin Platonic philosopher, describes in his *Metamorphoses*, or *The Golden Ass*, the initiation in the Mysteries of Isis of one Lucius Patras, now uniformly believed to be Apuleius himself:

> Hear, then, and believe, for what I tell is true. I drew nigh to the confines of death, I trod the threshold of Proserpine [Hades], I was borne through all the elements and returned to earth again. I saw the sun gleaming with bright splendour at dead of night, I approached the gods above, and the gods below, and worshipped them face to face. Behold, I have told thee things of which, though thou hast heard them, thou must yet know naught.
>
> I will recount, therefore, only that which may without sin be imparted to the understanding of the uninitiate. So soon as it was morning and the rites were accomplished, I came forth clothed in the twelve cloaks that are worn by the initiate, a raiment that is most holy. . . . The precious cloak hung from my shoulders down my back, even to my heels, and I was adorned, wheresoever thou mightest cast thine eye, with the figures of beasts broidered round about in diverse colours.* . . . This cloak the initiates call the cloak of Olympus. In my right hand I bore a torch

*The reference to the twelve cloaks and the figures of beasts suggests the mystic passage through the twelve signs of the zodiac.

flaming with fire, and my head was garlanded with a fair crown of spotless palm, whose leaves stood out like rays . . . adorned as the sun and set up like to the image of a god.

> — quoted by Lewis Spence, *The Mysteries of Egypt*, pp. 70–1

In the Greater Mysteries, the passage into the underworld ceases to be a mere ritual of the Lesser Mysteries in which the candidate participates. He must now approach "the confines of death" with full knowledge, and in the garment of soul-consciousness pass beyond the veil of visible nature into the arena of worlds invisible:

It is one of the fundamental teachings of occultism that nothing can be *truly known* which is not *experienced, lived through.* . . . different stages or degrees of initiation are really a kind of forcing-process, for certain chosen spirits, certain chosen souls, who have proved themselves worthy: . . . These different stages or degrees of initiation are marked by preparatory purifications, first. Then came the "death," a mystic death. The body and lower principles, so to say, are paralyzed, and the soul is temporarily freed. And, to a certain extent, the freed inner man is guided and directed and helped by the initiators while it passes into other spheres and to other planes and learns the nature

of these *by becoming them,* which is the only way
by which knowledge thereof roots itself into the soul,
into the ego: by *becoming the thing.*

— FEP, pp. 258–9

This mystic death constitutes the fourth initiation,
which consists not only in one's ability to receive spiritual light, but likewise in one's power to face with
equanimity and awakened morality the darkness of
evil. To *become a thing* is actually to unite one's cog-
nizing intelligence with the essence of that being or
thing; in other words, to *take on the nature* of such
entity for the time being. Hence, to weld one's consciousness with beings in spheres *lower* than the human is greatly to test the stamina of the individual:
will the malefic fumes of the lower spheres stifle the
delicate petals of the budding adept? Will the sen-
suous delights of the lower hells have any attraction for
the neophyte stern in his resolve? Conversely, to as-
sume the nature of beings in spheres *higher* than the
human calls for an equally tempered constitution: will
the brilliance and splendor of truth undimmed blind
the soul? Will vision of reality shatter the awakening
eye of wisdom?

This fourth degree may be considered a prelude to,
a minor reflection of, the final and seventh degree of
initiation in which the individual must undergo the

trial of identification with *all* spheres of being. To complete the full initiatory cycle, therefore, demands the awakening and strengthening of *all seven* human principles. The candidate must have so tuned his seven-stringed lyre, so energized it with spiritual harmony, that it will vibrate in perfect synchrony with the *spiritual* essence of the seven principles or spheres of the cosmos. As Master KH wrote in 1882 to Allan O. Hume of Simla, India: "The degrees of an Adept's initiation mark the seven stages at which he discovers the secret of the sevenfold principles in nature and man and awakens his dormant powers" (*ML*, Letter xv, p. 99).

Of these higher degrees scarcely anything is known to us. This is natural, and indeed appropriate; for how could words describe that which can be understood only by the initiate? How could that which is essentially esoteric be revealed and still retain its mystic integrity? Important hints, however, have been given regarding the fifth, sixth, and seventh degrees.

In the fifth initiation, the initiant *"meets his own god-self face to face*, and for a longer or shorter time *becomes one with it"* (*FEP*, p. 283). This degree was called by the Greeks *theophany*, a word signifying "divine appearance" or "showing forth of a divinity," the appearance or manifestation of man's own higher self to himself. And while in the average candidate this sublime moment of intellectual ecstasis and high vision lasted but a short time, with further spiritual progress of the candidate the theophanic communion became more enduring and lasting, until finally, ultimately, man knew himself, not merely as the offspring spiritually of his own inner god, but as that inner god itself, in his essential being.

— *FEP*, p. 447

The sixth initiation was consummated as the inevitable course of events following upon the successful spiritualization of the entire nature. This was called *theopneusty* by the Greeks — a word literally signifying "god-breathing" or "divine inspiration" — where the disciple

felt the inbreathing from his own inner god and became, thus, inspired, the very word inspiration meaning "inbreathing." With the passing of time and the greater purification of the soul-vehicle, which is man himself, this inbreathing or inspiration became permanent. — Ibid.

In this degree "the inner god of the candidate breathes down into him, for a longer or shorter time, depending upon his advancement, the wisdom and the knowledge of all the universe . . ."; and "in the sixth degree, instead of one's own Higher Self, the initiant meets another One, . . ." (*FEP*, pp. 284, 260).

Then comes the seventh and last of the degrees of initiation before masterhood is achieved. This initiation usually took place at the winter solstice. The ancient pagan initiates considered the four points of the year, the winter and summer solstices and the spring and autumnal equinoxes, as representative of holy workings in the cosmos. The birth of the sun at the beginning of the year symbolized to them the mystic birth of the initiate, and it is significant that nearly all the great world saviors, such as Jesus the Christ, Krishna the Avatāra, Apollonius of Tyana, and others, celebrate their "birthdays" at this sacred time: the rebirth of the solar deity.

This seventh degree, which is called *theopathy* — a Greek word meaning "god-suffering" or "divine-enduring" — is the

> most sublime mystery of all, . . . the initiant, the candidate, suffered himself to become, abandoned himself fully to be, a truly selfless channel of communication of his own inner god, his own higher self; he became lost as it were in the greater self of his own higher self.   — *FEP*, p. 447

Few indeed are those whose soul strength is so

great that they can suffer in fullness the presence of divinity. This is the reward of the highest adepts, those whose sacrifice and wisdom surround humanity with a guardian wall diamond-like in compassion and protection.

In the seventh degree, the neophyte passes the portals of the sun; *"he becomes for a passing moment the Wondrous Watcher himself"* (*FEP*, p. 260). The solar initiation is complete: the neophyte dies, and the hierophant is born.

Chapter 9

Routes of Initiation

IN THE DEEPER MYSTERY-TRAINING, the pupil must not only learn to build the mystic vessel of awakened consciousness which will carry him from plane to plane but, in the process of such individual becoming, must rediscover for himself the ageless routes of initiation.

In wisdom and foresight, nature is consistent throughout: one law, one plan, one structure. With charming thrift she rehearses the pathways of initiation through the cycles of sleep and death. Death and its processes form the heart and core of the Greater Mysteries: through death of the inferior the superior finds birth. Except the seed die, the flower cannot bloom; except the flower die, the seed cannot form. "He that loseth his life for my sake shall find it" (*Matt.* 10:39).

Sleep is an incomplete death — unconsciously experienced; death is a complete sleep — unconsciously experienced; initiation is a self-conscious sleep or "death" of the lower elements with a fully conscious liberation of the spiritual soul along the pathways of sleep and death.

In sleep the body "dies" imperfectly, for the golden cord remains linked to the slumbering body. If the soul is not weighted with material desire, then a natural quiescence ensues. During the brief hours of nightly sleep, if the karma be favorable the freed spirit-soul may ascend out of the sphere of earth along the invisible magnetic pathways to higher realms. The ascent is instantaneous, followed by the return along identic pathways until the soul once again enters the sleeping body and a new day dawns.

The pathways of sleep traversed night after night constitute an *unconscious* journey along the routes of initiation. Such momentary and unrecognized contact during sleep is not wasted; the very repetition of the selfsame process acts as an invisible spur to the ordinary person. If the aspirations continue and the life is made purer, faint impressions of beauty and grandeur will penetrate the soul, intuitions will manifest, and the aspirant will find benediction sweeping into his days through nightly communion with higher spheres.

Death is the following of the same processes of

sleep, only perfectly so. The body is cast off permanently and dissipates; the golden cord is withdrawn, and the soul, freed of its terrestrial elements, enters the spheres of temporary purgation. Liberated and cleansed of earthly dross, the soul ascends to its spiritual parent, the higher self, and in peace and bliss undreamed of pursues the identic journey of sleep. In each of the mansions of space, a stop is made, shorter or longer depending upon the links of affinity formerly made through past experience of the spiritual soul until, strengthened by divine contact, it once again treads the ancient pathway, and a child is born on earth.

Thus in death the age-old routes of initiation are followed by the spiritual monad in conscious recognition, but as yet in unconscious appreciation by the ordinary human soul.

A human being is many-sided: he has within him a divine monad, a spiritual soul, and a human soul which works through his vital-astral-physical nature. We must guard against the lower gaining dominion over the higher and must watch carefully, particularly in discussion of these holy themes, lest we become so fascinated by their beauty and intellectual splendor, that we forget their essential worth — that of ethics. Unless an individual has made ethics the foundation of his character, his heart and mind will be continually shaken by the storms of desire.

Those who care for little beyond the immediate will have scant attraction to deeper things, but those who have begun to think and feel intuitively may find themselves irresistibly drawn to the ancient wisdom. However, to those already stirring from the sleep of matter, warning is repeatedly given against entertaining the notion that initiation is just around the corner. One must defend the heart against selfish desire for so-called occult powers as one would defend oneself against the bite of a serpent. The initiations referred to, more particularly in the previous chapter, are not described but only alluded to as hints of what some day the worthy disciple may find himself fortunate enough to experience.

In summation, over and over the journey of initiation is traversed: in sleep imperfectly, in death more perfectly; nightly by the soul in sleep, periodically by the soul in death. Unconsciously undergone, nature thus rehearses that which the soul must one day follow with will and consciousness fully active. This latter process is the journey of initiation: the deliberate paralysis of terrestrial influence followed by the self-perceptive journey through every plane and sphere of the cosmos.

In his *Esoteric Tradition*, Purucker elaborates:

> The purpose of the passing of the Monad post-mortem through the various planetary chains is to allow it to free itself on each such planetary chain of the integument or habiliment or vehicle which belongs to the vital essence of such planetary chain. It is only thus that the Monad strips off from itself one after the other the different "coatings" with which it has enwrapped itself during its long evolutionary journey; and thus when it has freed itself from all the seven "coatings" it is then ready, because freed and in its pure and "unclothed" state, to enter into its own native spiritual Home. When the return journey towards Earth's planetary chain begins, the Monad then passes through all these same seven planets, but in reverse order to that by which it had ascended through them, and in each such planet that it visits . . . it picks up and re-assumes or clothes itself in the life-atoms forming the "coatings" that it had previously dropped or cast off in each one of these seven planets respectively. — 2:869–70

So important is this journey that the Greater Mysteries dealt almost entirely with processes of the mystic death. As stated in the previous chapter, the fourth initiation comprised a partial descent into lower spheres, accompanied by a partial ascent into superior spheres. The soul as yet has not developed sufficient strength to withstand the full revelation of the universe.

There is a Babylonian legend which points to a Mystery-teaching. Ishtar* descends to the underworld and, arriving at the gates of Arallu (Hades), stands beautiful and regal. The archaic decree, however, demands that none may enter the dread precincts of the underworld who are not bare of garment or jewel.

> Therefore at each of the successive gates through which Ishtar must pass, the keeper divests her of some garment or ornament: first her crown, then her earrings, then her necklace, then the ornaments from her bosom, then her many-jeweled girdle, then the spangles from her hands and feet, and lastly her loin-cloth.
> — Will Durant, *The Story of Civilization* 1:238

Free and pure she enters the Land of No Return where her sister, Ereshkigal, holds sway. Full of jealousy, she sends against Ishtar sixty diseases. Having passed the tests of the lower world, Ishtar retraces her steps through the seven gates, receiving in reverse order the garments and jewels which she had cast aside on her descending journey, and finally, as she ascends into the regions of light, Ishtar is adorned with the seventh jewel, the crown of spiritual glory.

---

*A variant of the Sumerian Inanna.

The descent to the underworld is not an automatic process, but a willing decision to undertake the journey as a supreme test of intellectual and spiritual integrity. If the candidate succeed, union with the divine and bliss supernal will be his; if he fail, then death or madness lies in store. Far better had he never ventured upon these trials, for fearful indeed are they. But all is not lost, for in a future life he may try again.

If the aspirant has through austerity, utter devotion, discipline, and learning become as gold in the fire, swift and sure will be his passage through the lower worlds. With the flame of spirituality burning within, the successful candidate rises to the spheres superior, where the passage from planet to planet is made with full awareness. Passing the ultimate test, the pupil, now become master, returns to earth and to his entranced body.

The guardian of the initiation chamber, who has watched over the body of his disciple with patient and loving care, is filled with joy: the initiation is consummated.

Chapter 10

The Closing of the Mystery Schools

FIFTEEN CENTURIES AGO the death knell of the Mysteries in the West sounded when Emperor Theodosius II banished paganism from the Roman Empire, which at that time included Thrace, Macedonia, Crete, Syria, and Egypt. The final blow came less than a century later, in 529 AD, when Emperor Justinian closed the last philosophical school of Athens, the Academy founded by Plato. Aside from the suppression of everything non-Christian, much of what had once been held beautiful and holy in the Mysteries — the sacred ritual of the union of the aspiring soul with the higher self — had become orgies of the most degraded sort.

Never in the history of occultism, past or present, can it be said that the Mysteries — in their purity and spiritual integrity — cater to the personal and emotional nature. It is precisely to free the soul of limitation, to purify the heart and discipline the mind, that the Mystery training is so severe, for in initiation only spiritual strength, only diamond caliber can withstand the searching ordeal.

Birth, growth, maturity, and senescence are the inevitable processes of nature in all her departments. A Mystery school need not undergo a *degenerate* senescence, any more than a person's declining years need be marked by degradation. But, as with ourselves, the seeds of degeneracy and ambition are too frequently sown in the heyday of material success. Likewise with a genuine Mystery-center, if the challenge of spiritual growth is not met with ever greater austerity of heart than in days of probation, the venomous seeds of inner decay take root and grow. Degradation replaces quiescence, and the school decays. The spirit of the Brotherhood retreats, the rind of ritual remains.

The real cause, therefore, of the closing of the Mystery schools is the *inner faithlessness* of the guardians of the temple. Never would the light die out if the hierophants remained loyal to the timeless principles of the school, for the Brotherhood watches with eagle eye for every light, and when the call is strong and the cry for truth powerful, the Mysteries remain pure and true.

When the human race, or any branch of it, or even an individual, makes the spiritual and intellectual

appeal in terms so strong, with spiritual energy so
vibrant, with the very fiber of the inner life so to say,
it actually operates with the spiritual magnetism of a
Teacher, and the call is heard in the Great Brotherhood
invariably, and an Envoy or Messenger appears in the
world as its representative. The Mysteries have always
degenerated because men became involved more and
more in selfishness and the self-seeking ways of the
material world, and lost the inner touch, the inner
consciousness of communion with the spiritual Powers
mentioned above.   — *ET* 2:1053

There are two paths in occultism: the right-hand
path of white magic and spiritual progress; and the
left-hand path of black magic and spiritual retrogres-
sion. No third path of cessation or rest exists. If one
does not go forwards, then he will remain behind.
The stream of evolutionary progress is forwards, to-
ward the light of spirit and truth. If one does not
travel this path, he falls by the wayside; the caravan
moves on, the idler remains behind.

The further one proceeds on the path of esoteric
training, the sharper is the line of demarcation between these two paths; yet, paradoxically, just because
of the richer development of the disciple, the finer
sensitivity to right and wrong, the greater are the
depths sounded as well as the heights attained. The

middle line of wisdom becomes ever more elusive as progress in spiritual things is made. It is not the gross pitfalls of former lives that the pupil need guard against, but the subtle refinements of *Māra,* the "tempter," who with cruel and insidious measure tries the soul relentlessly.

An Eastern proverb says that between the "right and the left hand [magic] there is but a cobweb thread" (*BCW* 14:106). He who would remain on the path must cling with all his strength and courage to the cobweb thread of wisdom.

One of the most effective weapons of the dark forces is doubt — doubt of oneself, of one's aspirations and inherent strength. To doubt is a natural reaction of discipleship, but a highly dangerous state while it lasts. If not checked with stern resolve to keep on — no matter how often one falls or how grave the error — self-pity obtains mastery and the door to a graver peril is opened: doubt of the teacher, doubt of the school, doubt of the Brotherhood. Here flourishes the fatal seed of interior disarray which, if not cast out from the heart, will grow into the weed of infidelity.

Terrible are the tests of an aspirant to chelaship, and severe have been the warnings to the over-eager. As KH wrote to A. P. Sinnett in 1881:

> *those who engage themselves in the occult sciences . . .*
> "must either reach the goal or *perish.* Once fairly
> started on the way to the great Knowledge, to doubt is
> to risk insanity; to come to a dead stop is to fall; to
> recede is to tumble backward, headlong into an abyss."
> — *ML*, Letter VIII, p. 31

There are three results of initiation: (a) success; (b)
failure which means death; and (c) partial failure
which usually means madness (see *FEP*, p. 292). It is
for this reason that would-be chelas are repeatedly
warned against undue rushing into occultism. Far
safer to remain in the outer courts of the temple of
wisdom as earnest and sincere aspirants for greater
knowledge, as learners striving to practice the age-old
rules of the Sanctuary: loyalty, duty, and selfless fidelity to the cause of humanity. If these are cherished
and held to through the travail and heartache of human existence, the time will inevitably come when
help will be forthcoming, and the aspirant will know
that he has been "accepted." Until such time, wiser to
live a noble life in the position karma has ordained.

Unwise ardor for spiritual discipline, however, is
not half so dangerous as personal desire for occult training merely for self-gain. It was the overweening rush
for occult powers which laid the foundation for degen-
eration of the Mystery schools in the early centuries of

our era. For hundreds of years the Mysteries had been slowly losing their sanctity; too many had been received into the preliminary degrees not by virtue of inner development, but for temporal reasons. The rites became perfunctory observances, and perception of interior worth diminished. Dogma, ritual, and priestcraft waxed, the spirit of truth and esotericism waned. The few — all too few indeed — who had remained faithful to their sacred pledge fled the precincts of the Mysteries which in later Roman times had become so degenerate as actually to repel from their chambers those whose hearts sought only the genuinely esoteric.

The light was withdrawn, but so compassionately does the Brotherhood work that the truths have been preserved in symbol and stone, in allegory and mythos. As H. P. Blavatsky writes with respect to Egypt:

> Her sacred Scribes and Hierophants became wanderers upon the face of the earth. Those who had remained in Egypt found themselves obliged for fear of a profanation of the sacred Mysteries to seek refuge in deserts and mountains, to form and establish secret societies and brotherhoods — such as the Essenes; those who had crossed the oceans to India and even to the (now-called) New World, bound themselves by solemn oaths to keep silent, and to preserve secret their

Sacred Knowledge and Science; thus these were buried deeper than ever out of human sight. In Central Asia and on the northern borderlands of India, the triumphant sword of Aristotle's pupil swept away from his path of conquest every vestige of a once pure Religion: and its Adepts receded further and further from that path into the most hidden spots of the globe.

— *BCW* 14:294

Thus periodically is accomplished the work of the Brothers of the Shadow, the destruction of the *outposts* of the Mysteries, while the core and heart, the Brotherhood of Light, remains intact. Never will the hand of darkness lay hold upon the heart of esotericism which beats as strongly today as it did some 18 million years ago, and will continue to pulsate in undiminished power till the death of our solar system — and beyond. The light of truth is the light of the spiritual sun of our universe. As long as its rays gleam down into the world of earth, so long will the rays of spirit warm human hearts. In the stirring words of KH to A. O. Hume:

Fear not; . . . our knowledge will not pass away from the sight of man. It is the "gift of the gods" and the most precious relic of all. The keepers of the sacred Light did not safely cross so many ages but to find themselves wrecked on the rocks of modern scepticism. Our pilots are too experienced sailors to allow us [to] fear any such disaster. We will always find volunteers to replace the tired sentries, and the world, bad as it is in its present state of transitory period, can yet furnish us with a few men now and then.

— *ML*, Letter XXVIII, p. 215

Chapter 11

Line of Occult Succession

THE GREEKS WERE ADEPT in the use of imagery to convey profound esoteric truths, often using the form of sport; or, for instance, they would read into the exercises of the stadium inner significance. One of the best known examples of this was their portrayal through the torchbearer race of the mystic line of succession of great teachers.

> In the torch-race, the torch-bearer ran from post to post. On reaching the end of his stage he handed the lighted torch which he carried to the one there waiting, who immediately took up the race and in his turn handed it to the one waiting for him. This exercise of the arena or stadium was taken by many Greek and Latin writers as symbolizing the carrying on of Light from age to age, and as pointing to the spiritual Torch-bearers who pass the Torch of Truth from hand to hand throughout unending time.   — *ET* 2:1071

This handing on of the light of truth "throughout unending time" has formed the theme of many

Mystery parables. The Greeks also referred to this spiritual succession as the Golden Chain of Hermes which they believed to stretch far into the realms of Olympus, to "Father Zeus downwards through a series or line of spiritual beings and then through certain elect and lofty human beings to ordinary men" (*ET* 2:1070–1).

Purucker described this mystic succession as the *guruparamparā*. This is a Sanskrit compound literally meaning "teacher beyond beyond." The term signifies a line of teachers reaching beyond the beyond, through past, present, and into the distant future, whose sublime purpose is ever the same: the work of spiritualization.

> The ancient Mystery-Schools of every country of the globe and of whatever epoch in time, have had each one a Succession of Teachers trained and authorized by their training to teach in their turn; and as long as this transmission of the light of Truth was a reality in any one country, it was in every sense a truly spiritual institution. — *ET* 2:1071

An outstanding example of this ancient transmission is the succession of "living buddhas" of Tibet, which "is a real one, but of a somewhat special type, and it is by no means what Occidental scholars mistake it to be or have frequently misunderstood it to be" (*ET* 2:1071).

Further, in the Eleusinian Mysteries of Greece,

> hierophants were drawn from one family, the Eumolpidae, living in Athens, and the torchbearers were drawn from another family, the Lycomidae, living in Athens; and we have reason to believe that the Mysteries of Samothrace, the seat of an older rite, and which were, like the Mysteries of Eleusis, a State function, were also conducted in the same manner by the passing on of the tradition held sacred and incommunicable to outsiders; and the bond of union between the initiates of these so-called Mysteries was considered indissoluble, impossible of dissolution, for death merely strengthened the tie. — *FEP*, p. 287

In Persia as well as Egypt, we find this line of succession manifesting in another form. For example, there were the thirteen or more Zoroasters whose esoteric contribution to Persia's history was the inspiration of that once mighty civilization:

> The number of Zoroasters who have appeared from time to time is confusing, so long as we consider, and wrongly consider, these Zoroasters to be reimbodiments of one single ego, instead of different egos imbodying what we may interpret from the occult

records as the "Zoroaster-spirit." The truth of the matter is that in the scheme and terminology of Zoroastrianism, every Root-Race and sub-race, and minor race of the latter, has its own Zoroaster or Zoroasters. The term Zoroaster means in Zoroastrianism, very much what the term Buddha does in Buddhism, or Avatāra does in Brāhmanism. Thus there were great Zoroasters, and less Zoroasters — the qualificatory adjective depending upon the work done by each Zoroaster, and the sphere of things. Hence we can speak of the Zoroasters as being thirteen in number from one standpoint, or fourteen from another; or like the Manus in Brāhmanism, or like the Buddhas in Buddhism, we can multiply each of these by seven again, or even fourteen if we take in every little branchlet race with its guiding Zoroaster-spirit.   — *SOP,* p. 636

In Egypt, Hermes Trismegistus ("Hermes the thrice greatest") stands out from the long Hermes line, whose writings and teachings were founded on the ancient Mystery doctrine. In Greece also we find the Orphic Mysteries, from whose halls of esoteric instruction came forth many who bore the name of Orpheus.

What impelled these pupils to take the names of their teachers? Why did they sign their work, or give oral instruction, in the name of Orpheus, Hermes, or

Zoroaster? Was it a kind of spiritual plagiarism, or was it rather because of a compelling gratitude to the teacher who had given them ALL, who had lighted the flame of esoteric fire in their hearts? Surely the latter, for whatever message they had of inspiration and light they deemed not theirs, but "his who sent me" — "As we have received it, thus shall we pass it on." This practice is distressing to later historians who struggle always to attach correct labels to things, yet one cannot help but love these old disciples for that loyalty of soul which banishes all thought of *individual* greatness.

The relationship between disciple and teacher is a most sacred bond of spiritual intimacy. Gratitude wells up from the disciple commensurate with greatness of soul: the little of heart feel only resentment when guidance and protection are offered; but the large of heart burn with the flame of loving and inextinguishable gratitude. The links in this Golden Chain of Hermes are joined by gratitude. As each link is coupled with its brother link, heart with heart, teacher with pupil, pupil with teacher — each teacher a pupil to the one above, each pupil a teacher to the one below — all bonded by unbreakable links of love, fidelity, and gratitude to the teacher, to the Brotherhood, to the esoteric wisdom:

Like signal-fires of the olden times, which, lighted and extinguished by turns upon one hill-top after another, conveyed intelligence along a whole stretch of country, so we see a long line of "wise" men from the beginning of history down to our own times communicating the word of wisdom to their direct successors. Passing from seer to seer, the "Word" flashes out like lightning, and while carrying off the initiator from human sight forever, brings the new initiate into view.

— *Isis* 2:571

This "long line of 'wise' men" has been kept unbroken since the middle of the third root-race by two methods: (a) the actual reincarnation of adepts, and (b) the birth of the initiate out of the disciple. In this way the Brotherhood revitalizes its membership through the rebirth of hierophants, and the "second birth" of recruits from the ranks of the Mystery chambers (see *ET* 2:1070). The "Passing of the Word" was the final rite of the solar initiation: without it no transmission of occult authority could be made from initiator to disciple.

Hence the line of esoteric authority and wisdom advances in serial order through grade after grade of chelaship to the adepts; from adepts to high mahatmas; from high mahatmas to buddhas; from buddhas to dhyāni-buddhas; from dhyāni-buddhas to the spiritual guide and protector of the planetary chain of earth; from the earth planetary spirit to the heart of the sun. Truly a line of luminous glory linking the humblest of disciples of wisdom with the solar logos.

Chapter 12

The Mystery Schools of Today

THE BROTHERHOOD OF GREAT ONES never deserts humanity. Underneath and behind and within there pulsates the eternal heart of compassion. Withdrawal of the Mystery schools from public knowledge by no means indicates withdrawal of the perennial support of the Mahatmas. Mystery-centers are to be found today all over the world, writes H. P. Blavatsky, for "the Secret Association is still alive and as active as ever" (*Isis* 2:100). Guarded with jealous care by their protectors, the precise location of these schools is undiscoverable except by the worthy; however, a veil of secrecy is not synonymous with nonexistence.

Does the physical body remain alive and functional if the heart ceases to pump blood into the circulatory system, if the organs do not receive their vital flow from the heart? Thus with the spiritual body of the earth, whose mystic heart is Śambhala, and from whose ventricles flows forth into organic centers the esoteric life-blood of the Brotherhood. Every Mystery-center is an organic focus, every human being is a living cell. All owe spiritual allegiance to the central heart. Is it logical to infer that a heart beats in vain? Is it logical to infer that organs function apart from the heart? Such conclusions are against reason or experience.

Three are the distributions, therefore, of this esoteric life-flow:

(1) Through the exoteric and the esoteric Mysteries. The exoteric or Lesser Mysteries are now "largely replaced by the different activities of the Theosophical Movement which itself is exoteric as a Movement" (*SOP*, p. 637). The esoteric or Greater Mysteries, because of the weight of matter blinding the world-consciousness, are at present far more carefully hid. Significantly, just because of the increased need for light and truth, "the esoteric groups of Mystery-Schools are perhaps more numerous today than they have been for thousands of years, . . ." (ibid.).

This fact is of far-reaching importance for seekers after truth. Once the power and force of the ancient wisdom seizes the citadel of the heart, one may receive not only genuine spiritual uplift through contact with the exoteric Mysteries but, more importantly, he places himself in direct line of inspiration from the esoteric Mysteries, the seats or organic centers of the Brotherhood.

(2) Through organic foci of national compass. In the circulation of spiritual influences all countries are in magnetic and sympathetic vibration with Śambhala. Every great country has its esoteric centers:

Thus a little country like The Netherlands might be the center of a secret Mystery-School whose ramifications and influence would extend over half of Europe . . . Yet as a matter of fact, every single National unit of the globe, has its own secret spiritual protectors, who as a body form a true esoteric center. We can call these the Occult Guardians of a people. Thus Britain has hers, Germany has hers, Russia has hers, likewise so with Switzerland, France, Italy, Spain, Portugal, China, India, Japan, the United States, Mexico, Canada, Brazil, etc., etc., etc. — Ibid.

These national occult guardians do not meddle in political affairs; their work is "purely spiritual, moral, intellectual, and wholly benevolent, and indeed universal, and is a silent guide to the intuitive minds of the different races" (ibid., p. 638).

(3) The third channel of esoteric work is one of the most fascinating, yet least recognized: that of preserving the knowledge from age to age.

There are actually groups whose sole business is forming occult centers of Initiation, preparation of students for esoteric work in the world, and for the safeguarding of priceless treasures, the heirlooms of the human race, treasures both intellectual and material.

— *SOP*, p. 637

The generations of seers are not wasteful, nor are the grand systems of philosophy and religion lost in the darkness of receding ages. All that is of essential spiritual value is preserved in the secret archives of the planet:

There are, scattered throughout the world, a handful of thoughtful and solitary students, who pass their lives in obscurity, far from the rumors of the world, studying the great problems of the physical and spiritual universes. They have their secret records in which are preserved the fruits of the scholastic labors of the long line of recluses whose successors they are. The knowledge of their early ancestors, the sages of India, Babylonia, Nineveh, and the imperial Thebes; the legends and traditions commented upon by the masters of Solon, Pythagoras, and Plato, in the marble halls of Heliopolis and Saïs; traditions which, in their days, already seemed to hardly glimmer from behind the foggy curtain of the past; — all this, and much more, is recorded on indestructible parchment, and passed with jealous care from one adept to another.

— *Isis* 1:557–8

Some day worthy explorers will recover the lost keys, and mystery after mystery will be solved; temples will be unearthed; secrets of the initiatory chambers revealed; the occult history of the planet and human races unfolded. When? At the appointed hour, an hour not fixed by whim or fancy, but brought into being as the third eye now "most carefully hidden and inaccessible" opens once again in esoteric birth.

According to Purucker, the chief of these hid centers has its home in Śambhala, with branches in Syria, Mexico, Egypt, the United States, and Europe, each one "subordinate to the mother-group of the Occult Hierarchy in Śambhala" (*SOP*, p. 637).

In *The Mahatma Letters* a wonderful description is given by Master M of a secret retreat in which his brother and friend KH enters the silence of further initiation. Masters, though vastly superior to us, are still human beings — grandly human, but human nevertheless — and must undergo further testing, but such initiations are of supernal character. Of the trial of his co-worker, Master M writes:

> Two days later when his [KH's] "retreat" was decided upon in parting he asked me: "Will you watch over my work, will you see it falls not into ruins?" I promised. What is there I would not have promised him at that hour! At a certain spot not to be men-

tioned to outsiders, there is a chasm spanned by a frail bridge of woven grasses and with a raging torrent beneath. The bravest member of your Alpine clubs would scarcely dare to venture the passage, for it hangs like a spider's web and *seems* to be rotten and impassable. Yet it is not; and he who dares the trial and succeeds — as he will if it is right that he should be permitted — comes into a gorge of surpassing beauty of scenery — to one of *our* places and to some of *our* people, of which and whom there is no note or minute among European geographers. At a stone's throw from the old Lamasery stands the old tower, within whose bosom have gestated generations of Bodhisatwas. It is there, where now rests your lifeless friend . . .

— Letter XXIX, p. 219

There within the Sanctuary are "gestated generations of Bodhisattvas," among whose esoteric purposes is the enlightenment of humanity. Through all the heartache and sorrow of the world, this strong network of occult vitality flows in unceasing rhythm along the invisible arteries and veins of the body spiritual of our earth. So profound is the compassion of the Brotherhood, so untiring its labor, that not until the heartbeat of every human being shall pulsate in harmony with the heartbeat of the Great Brotherhood will it lay down its task.

Sources and Abbreviations

Apuleius, *The Isis-Book* (*Metamorphoses Book XI*), ed. and trans. J. Gwyn Griffiths, E. J. Brill, Leiden, 1975.

——, *Metamorphoses, or The Golden Ass,* quoted in Lewis Spence, *The Mysteries of Egypt.* See also *Transformation of Lucius Otherwise Known as The Golden Ass,* trans. Robert Graves, Farrar, Straus & Giroux, New York, 1951.

ML Barker, A. Trevor, comp., *The Mahatma Letters to A. P. Sinnett,* 2nd edition, T. Fisher Unwin, London, 1926; facsimile edition, Theosophical University Press, Pasadena, 1992.

BCW Blavatsky, H. P., *Collected Writings,* compiled by Boris de Zirkoff, 15 vols., Theosophical Publishing House, Wheaton, Madras [Chennai], London, 1958–1991.

Isis ——, *Isis Unveiled: A Master-Key to the Mysteries of Ancient and Modern Science and Theology,* 2 vols., J. W. Bouton, New York; Bernard Quaritch, London, 1877; reprint, Theosophical University Press, Pasadena, 1999.

SD ——, *The Secret Doctrine: The Synthesis of Science, Religion, and Philosophy,* 2 vols., The Theosophical Publishing Co., Ltd., London, New York, Madras, 1888; facsimile edition, Theosophical University Press, Pasadena, 1999.

———, *The Theosophical Glossary*, The Theosophical Publishing Society, London, 1892; facsimile edition, Theosophy Company, Los Angeles, 1990.

———, *The Voice of the Silence*, The Theosophical Publishing Co., Ltd, London, New York, Madras 1889; verbatim reprint, Theosophical University Press, Pasadena, 1994.

Durant, Will, *The Story of Civilization*, Vol. 1, *Our Oriental Heritage*, Simon and Schuster, New York, 1935.

Eliade, Mircea, *A History of Religious Ideas*, Vol. 1, *From the Stone Age to the Eleusinian Mysteries*, trans. Willard R. Trask, University of Chicago Press, Chicago, 1978.

Ginsburg, Christian D., D.D., *The Kabbalah: Its Doctrines, Development and Literature*, George Routledge & Sons, London, 1925; reprinted with *The Essenes: Their History and Doctrines*, Macmillan Company, New York, 1956.

Judge, William Q., *The Bhagavad-Gita combined with Essays on the Gita* (Recension), Theosophical University Press, Pasadena, 1969.

Kanta, Katherine G., *Eleusis: Myth, Mysteries, History, Museum*, trans. W. W. Phelps, The National Museum, Athens, 1979.

Kerényi, Carl, *Eleusis: Archetypal Image of Mother and Daughter*, trans. Ralph Manheim, Bollingen Series LXV · 4, Pantheon Books, New York, 1967.

Meyer, Marvin W., ed., *The Ancient Mysteries: A Sourcebook, Sacred Texts of the Mystery Religions of the Ancient Mediterranean World,* Harper & Row, San Francisco, 1987.

Mylonas, George E., *Eleusis and the Eleusinian Mysteries,* Princeton University Press, Princeton, 1961.

The Mysteries: Papers from the Eranos Yearbooks, Bollingen Series XXX · 2, Pantheon Books, New York, 1955.

Oliver, George, D.D., *The History of Initiation,* Macoy Publishing and Masonic Supply Co., New York, 1923.

Pert Em Hru (Egyptian *Book of the Dead*), various editions.

ET   Purucker, G. de, *The Esoteric Tradition,* 2nd edition, Theosophical University Press, Point Loma, 1940; reprint, Pasadena, 1973.

FEP   ———, *Fundamentals of the Esoteric Philosophy,* 2nd and revised edition, Theosophical University Press, Pasadena, 1979.

SOP   ———, *Studies in Occult Philosophy,* Theosophical University Press, Covina, 1945; reprint, Pasadena, 1973.

Spence, Lewis, *The Mysteries of Egypt, or The Secret Rites and Traditions of the Nile,* Rider & Co., London, [1933].

Sūrya-Siddhānta: A Text-Book of Hindu Astronomy, trans. Rev. Ebenezer Burgess (and W. D. Whitney), American Oriental Society, New Haven, 1860; reprint, Wizards Bookshelf, San Diego, 1978.

Theon of Smyrna, *Mathematics Useful for Understanding Plato*, trans. Robert and Deborah Lawlor, Wizards Bookshelf, San Diego, 1979.

The Vishnu Purāna, trans. H. H. Wilson, edited by Fitz-Edward Hall, 5 vols. plus index, Trübner & Co., London, 1864–77.

Index